Great Ideas of Science

ELECTRICITY
AND
MAGNETISM

by Peter Fairley

Twenty-First Century Books
Minneapolis

*To my big brother Gerard
and to the budding physicists and engineers who must
reinvent our energy systems in the decades to come*

Twenty-First Century Books
A division of Lerner Publishing Group, Inc.
241 First Avenue North
Minneapolis, Minnesota 55401 U.S.A.

Website address: www.lernerbooks.com

537
FAI

Library of Congress Cataloging-in-Publication Data

Fairley, Peter, 1967–
    Electricity and magnetism / by Peter Fairley.
      p. cm. — (Great ideas of science)
    Includes bibliographical references and index.
    ISBN-13: 978–0–8225–6605–2 (lib. bdg. : alk. paper)
    1. Electricity—Juvenile literature. 2. Magnetism—Juvenile
literature. I. Title.
    QC527.2.F35 2008
    537—dc22   2006029923

Manufactured in the United States of America
1 2 3 4 5 6 – DP – 13 12 11 10 09 08

TABLE OF CONTENTS

INTRODUCTION

Imagine you are walking along a lakeshore on a cool fall night when the sky suddenly explodes. Shimmering bands of iridescent color tower overhead. Celestial warriors sweep down from the heavens, their mighty weapons raised.

That is just how a Tlingit Indian living along North America's northwestern coast hundreds of years ago might have described the auroras. These colored lights descend from Earth's polar regions. Without warning, the black of the night sky is streaked with red, yellow, green, purple, and blue. Minutes or hours later, the displays disappear just as mysteriously as they came. The aurora borealis, better known as the northern lights, paints the sky in the Northern Hemisphere. The aurora australis lights up the southern sky.

For thousands of years, people imagined that gods or demons created the auroras. Many thought they saw animated figures dancing or jumping in another world. The

Tlingit believed the lights were the spirits of dead warriors, locked in eternal battle. The Inuit of Greenland and northeastern Canada believed the flickering lights were ancestors seeking to contact their living kin. Whistle to the lights, thought the Inuit, and you might reach dead relatives.

Still other peoples imagined the lights to be the reflection of great fires. The Maori tribes of the South Pacific thought the auroras were fires lit as rescue beacons by lost Maori trapped in icy lands to the south.

We no longer explain the auroras as ghosts or flames. Instead, we recognize them as by-products of electricity interacting with Earth's magnetism. Like all forms of electricity, the auroras result from the movement of electrons. Electrons are the negatively charged particles in atoms.

The scientific study of electricity and magnetism began in earnest in the 1600s. It has unraveled some of life's greatest mysteries: the auroras, the beating of the human heart, and even the twisting of time and space known as relativity. It has also given rise to a wide range of technology. Electricity and magnetism encode the songs on your iPod, compress refrigerants to keep your ice cream from melting, and even print the words on this page.

Strap yourself in, because the story of electricity and magnetism moves fast. It goes all the way to the speed of light.

CHAPTER 1

ANCIENT ATTRACTION

Electricity and magnetism are ancient concepts. Electricity owes its name to a natural substance, amber. The Greek word for this fossilized tree sap is *elektron*.

In northern Europe, archaeologists have discovered 9,000-year-old animal carvings made of amber. They are among the oldest artistic objects ever found. People in southern Europe began to import amber beads from northern Europe at least 3,600 years ago.

Ancient Greeks valued amber as much as gold. Amber gleams like the Sun, is light enough to float, and feels warm to the touch. It also exhibits a strange power of attraction. When amber is rubbed, a static charge builds up on its surface. This charge can attract lightweight objects, such as bits of straw or feathers. A balloon rubbed on hair attracts lightweight objects; rubbed amber does too.

Amber's attraction was familiar to the ancient Greek philosopher Pliny the Elder (A.D. 23–79). Pliny wrote a treatise called *Natural History* in A.D. 70. In it he observed,

"When a vivifying heat has been imparted to it by rubbing it between the fingers, amber will attract chaff, dried leaves, and thin bark, just in the same way that the magnet attracts iron." Amber's mystical legacy endures. Some Roman Catholics own sacramental rosary beads—strings of beads that lead worshippers through prayers. Many Catholics rub a string of rosary beads as they seek comfort or inspiration. Those who use amber beads receive immediate electrical feedback!

MAGNETISM

The term *magnetism* also traces back to the ancient Greeks. It derives from Magnesia, a region of Greece's Mediterranean coast. There the ancient Greeks mined a silvery gray mineral called magnetite. Magnetite is a natural magnet.

According to Pliny's *Natural History*, a shepherd discovered magnetite's strange powers of attraction. Pliny wrote that this shepherd walked over an exposed vein of magnetite and suddenly found himself unable to move. The nails in his shoes and the iron tip of his staff had stuck fast to the magnetite.

In Pliny's day, some people thought a material that could push or pull something without touching it must be magical. Others thought it must be alive. Thales of Miletus, an ancient Greek philosopher and mathematician, believed that magnetite possessed a soul.

Architects of ancient Greece and Rome built magnetite bricks into the ceilings of temples. Iron figurines of rulers, gods, and mythical beasts were placed below them.

Thanks to the magnetic bricks, the iron models seemed to float in midair, inspiring awe in temple visitors.

The Chinese designed the first magnetic compass more than two thousand years ago. It employed a magnetite carving shaped like a short-handled spoon. The carving balanced atop a bronze dish. Fortune-tellers used the compass to determine the luckiest placement for everything from furniture and buildings to burial sites.

By the 1100s, the magnetic compass was common in Europe. Before the compass, sailors who dared to go beyond sight of shore took their bearing from the stars. When clouds or fog obscured the stars, they followed the wind. This was a risky proposition, given the wind's tendency to shift direction. The magnetic compass was much more reliable. It functioned as a substitute for Polaris, which we call the North Star. Because early mariners called Polaris the lodestar, the magnetite needle of early compasses earned the name "lodestone."

European compass builders used an iron needle, rather than magnetite, to make a lighter, more sensitive compass. First they magnetized the needle by laying it beside a block of magnetite. Then they positioned the needle atop a piece of cork or a wooden reed and floated it in water so it could turn freely.

Even as European mariners used magnetite, they remained wary of it. As late as the 1600s, mariners told fearful tales of magnetite's powers. One legend warned of magnetite-rich rocks in the Indian Ocean. The rocks were said to pull the nails out of ships, turning mighty vessels into floating wrecks.

This postage stamp features the magnetic compass designed by the ancient Chinese.

HEALING ROCKS

For many centuries, both amber and magnetite were thought to possess healing powers. Physicians prescribed amber for a wide range of ailments including coughs, nosebleeds, congested lungs, stomach illnesses, and even madness. They believed that rubbing magnetite on skin could draw illness out of the body.

The magical thinking began to change in 1600. A textbook on magnetism published that year set science on a very different course. Based on disciplined observation of both magnetism and static electricity, this book began to peel away fiction from fact.

COMPASS Before the invention of the magnetic compass,
CONFUSION mariners struggled to set a course whenever
clouds or fog hid the stars. The compass enabled
them to travel farther. But it was not perfect. Sailors soon
discovered that a compass needle rarely points due north.

Our planet's magnetism is believed to arise from the
movement of molten metal and rock deep inside Earth. As
these currents shift, so does Earth's magnetism. As a result, a
compass needle's deviation from true north—its declination—
differs from place to place and wanders over time.

British astronomer Edmond Halley, best known for the comet
that bears his name, set sail in 1698 on the first transoceanic
voyage specifically aimed at scientific research. Along the way,
he made frequent measurements of magnetic declination on
the Atlantic and Indian oceans. Upon returning home, Halley
made detailed declination charts. But he quickly learned that
such charts need frequent updating. Magnetic declination shifts
at different rates in different spots, so declination charts
quickly become inaccurate.

Another round of compass confusion began in the 1800s, with the
first iron ships. Sailors discovered the hard way that an iron ship
was itself a magnet, so it could throw off compass readings. As a
ship changed direction, so did its impact on the compass needle.

By mid-century compass designers and mariners were carefully
positioning small magnets around ships' compasses to cancel
out the ships' magnetism. When a ship's magnetism pulled the
compass needle in one direction, the small magnets around it
pulled the needle the other way. With the ship's magnetism
canceled out, Earth's magnetism once again controlled the
compass needle's direction.

CHAPTER 2

CAPTURING CHARGE

In 1600 William Gilbert, royal physician to Britain's Queen Elizabeth I, published a treatise on magnetism and static electricity called *On the Magnet*. He aimed to lift the fog of superstition surrounding magnets. He carefully observed their behavior and distinguished it from similar phenomena, particularly the attractive abilities of amber.

Many philosophers of Gilbert's day used magnetite and amber to explain anything they didn't understand. In contrast, Gilbert painstakingly observed and experimented on magnets and amber. In *On the Magnet*, he explained his experiments. The book set the stage for the development of modern electromagnetic science.

When Gilbert set to work, little was known about magnets except the simplest facts. Each magnet has two poles. When two magnets are brought together, like poles repel and unlike poles attract. One can induce (bring about) magnetism in iron by placing it close to a magnet.

Gilbert expanded the understanding of magnets by inventing two new devices.

One of Gilbert's inventions was a spherical lodestone. He called the magnet a terrella, which means "little Earth." Gilbert moved a compass over the terrella. He observed that the compass needle always lined up with the magnet's poles, just as a navigational compass always pointed roughly north-south.

He also noted that the needle increasingly tilted down, toward the surface of the sphere, as he moved the compass toward a pole. A navigational compass's needle also tilts this way as a ship sails north or south from the equator. The terrella experiments led Gilbert to a startling conclusion—Earth is a giant magnet.

Gilbert also used the terrella to explain induced magnetism. He observed that if he hung two nonmagnetized iron bars over the north pole of his terrella, they repelled each other. He realized that the terrella's magnetism had induced the iron bars to become weak magnets with the same orientation as the terrella—south pole down, north pole up. The bars repelled each other because they were hanging with like poles facing one another.

Gilbert called his second invention a versorium. This Latin word means "turn about." The versorium consisted of an iron needle rotating on a sharp metal point. For some of his experiments, Gilbert left the versorium's needle unmagnetized. For others, he magnetized the needle by rubbing it with a lodestone. Using the versorium, Gilbert proved that cutting a magnet in half produced two new magnets.

Gilbert also used the versorium to show that a magnet's pull multiplied as it approached the needle. When he decreased the distance between the magnet and the needle by half, the attraction more than doubled. He also showed that, in contrast to the accepted wisdom of the day, even the freshest garlic had no impact on a magnet's strength!

Gilbert devoted an entire chapter of *On the Magnet* to amber. In it, Gilbert showed how the attractive forces of amber and magnets differ. Prior to Gilbert's work, the two had often been confused.

To study amber's attractive properties, Gilbert loaded his versorium with a nonmagnetized needle. The iron needle responded to the static electricity on rubbed amber. Gilbert showed that many other materials, including diamond, glass, and wax, attracted the versorium's needle when he rubbed them with fur. Gilbert coined the term *electrics* to describe materials such as amber that excel at static cling. He noted that a broad range of objects could be made into electrics, but only those containing iron could become magnets.

Gilbert's versorium allowed him to demonstrate that magnets work the same in any weather, but rubbed amber gains greater charge in cold, dry weather. Dry air conducts static charges away from an object more slowly than air that is humid. This is why we get more static shocks in the winter.

On the Magnet also notes that a magnet's power of attraction and repulsion is concentrated at its poles. In contrast, the electric force radiates in all directions from a charged object such as rubbed amber.

ELECTRICAL FLUIDS

William Gilbert's *On the Magnet* sparked a revolution in science and technology, but it did not unfold as he hoped. Gilbert thought magnetism had much greater technological potential than electricity, but new applications of magnetism would not happen until the 1800s. In the meantime, Gilbert's observations on static electricity unleashed experimentation with the electric force.

By the late 1600s, people could buy hand-cranked machines to generate static charges. These electric generators built up a charge on a tube or sphere, usually made from sulfur or glass. Cranking the machine spun the tube or sphere. Pressing leather, silk, or wool against the spinning object created the friction needed to generate large amounts of static electricity. Like rubbed amber, the generator would hold its charge until it was discharged to another object or dissipated into the air.

Imagine rolling up your sleeves and cranking up your generator. Raising a metal rod to the charged object, you draw sparks like small lightning bolts. Now you ease your finger toward the charge. When it gets close enough, zap! The charge jumps to your hand, delivering a stinging shock.

At first these electrical generators were used for entertainment. Carnival showmen would charge up a sphere and amaze their audience with tiny bolts of lightning. Even professors took advantage of the devices' entertainment value. Georg Matthias Bose, a physicist at the University of Leipzig in Germany, electrified his dinner guests. Bose insulated the dinner table and his own chair from the ground by placing a nonelectric material such as glass under their legs. Then, at an opportune moment, he touched a wire from a hidden, fully charged static generator to the table. Sparks flew between the charged table and his guests' forks as they dug into their food.

Bose's trick worked because the electricity entering the table was drawn to the ground, where it would dissipate. To get there, the electricity couldn't travel down the legs of the table (or Bose's chair), which were grounded (insulated from the ground). Instead, it sparked across to the guests, through their chairs, and into the ground.

At first, university scientists thought of electricity as a trick and nothing more. It was considered unworthy of serious study. As a result, nonscientists performed some of the first careful experiments with static generators.

British cloth dyer Stephen Gray was a sixty-three-year-old retiree when he demonstrated the principles of electrical conduction in 1729. He did so by experimenting with combinations of materials that carry electricity and materials that do not. Gray suspended a metal wire from wooden poles. Near one end of the wire, he placed some brass flakes. At the other end, Gray charged up a glass tube.

MODERN USE OF GRAY'S TECHNIQUE Gray's greatest demonstration transmitted an electric charge 886 feet (270 meters). Modern electric power lines use Gray's principles to transmit electricity thousands of miles (kilometers). Ceramic or glass insulators between the wires and their towers keep the power hustling down the line rather than racing into the ground.

He touched the tube to the wire and watched the brass flakes. He saw no effect if he used another metal wire to suspend the wire. But if Gray suspended his wire with silk thread, the wire transferred the generator's charge. The static electricity made the flakes near the far end of the wire levitate (float upward).

Gray determined that there were two classes of materials—conductors, which can carry electricity, and insulators, which cannot. In his experiment, the wire that carried the charge was a conductor. If he hung it with metal wire—another conductor—the charge escaped before it reached the brass flakes. But when he suspended the wire with an insulator such as silk thread, the charge was transmitted to the other end.

In later demonstrations, Gray used another excellent conductor, the human body. Gray transmitted electricity through boys who were suspended from the ceiling. The boys transmitted the charge across a room by holding metal bars between them. Gray placed brass tinsel under the outstretched fingers of the boy on one end of the chain, then touched the boy on the other end with a charged glass rod. The charge was transmitted through the boys, levitating the tinsel. Such demonstrations became the rage in Europe.

While Gray and others transmitted electricity for entertainment, a retired French military officer used static generators to distinguish between two types of electrical charge. Charles-François de Cisternay DuFay performed his key experiments in 1733 and 1734. DuFay used a glass friction generator to charge a gold leaf. He observed that the charged leaf was repulsed by the glass but attracted to charged amber or wax.

DuFay explained the gold leaf's behavior by imagining two different fluids in the charged materials. The fluid that caused the charge on the glass he called vitreous, which is Latin for "glass." The fluid causing the charge on the amber and wax he called resinous, since it gathered in materials derived from resin (tree sap).

ELECTRIC CURRENT VERSUS ELECTRIC POWER

The static shocks delivered by Georg Matthias Bose and Stephen Gray were startling, but not dangerous. The electric currents unleashed by static electricity can carry as much voltage (the force that causes an electric current to flow, also known as electromotive force) as a high-voltage power line. However, they usually have a relatively low current (the number of electrons flowing per unit of time). As a result, static charges deliver little electric power, which depends on both current and voltage. In contrast, the electric sockets in your home provide an ample supply of electric current and, therefore, electric power. Hook up to that and you're asking for serious burns, loss of consciousness, and a potentially deadly scrambling of the electrical nerve impulses that regulate your heartbeat.

DuFay theorized that materials with an excess of the same fluid repelled one another, whereas materials with an excess of different fluids attracted one another. An object with vitreous charge would repel a second object with vitreous charge, just as a magnet's north pole repels another magnet's north pole. DuFay reasoned that the gold had picked up some of the vitreous fluid gathered on the glass, leaving both gold and glass in a vitreous state. Hence, they repelled one another. The rubbed amber, on the other hand, was full of resinous fluid. This fluid attracted the gold leaf's vitreous charge.

ELECTRICITY TO GO

Ten years after DuFay's experiments, the Leyden jar appeared on the scene. It was a new device for storing electricity. The Leyden jar couldn't be explained by DuFay's two-fluid theory. Scientists therefore had to change the way they thought about electricity.

The Leyden jar is a glass jar whose inner and outer surfaces are coated with metal foil. In the jar's mouth is a stopper made of an insulating material. A metal rod or chain is passed through the stopper and brought into contact with the jar's inner layer of foil. Early jars had no foil on the inside. Instead, they were filled with a liquid such as water. The liquid served to conduct charges from the metal rod to the inner surface of the jar.

The device takes its name from Leyden, Holland, where physicist Pieter van Musschenbroek stumbled upon the design in early 1746. But Ewald von Kleist, a cleric in Kamein, Poland (then part of Germany), had independently invented the device several months earlier.

Von Kleist came upon the design while trying to electrify water in a glass jar. DuFay had tried a similar experiment years earlier but failed because he had insulated the jar from the ground. In contrast, von Kleist held his jar while charging its fluid, so his jar was grounded. Grounding a Leyden jar allows charges to build up on the outside surface, thus drawing even more charges to the inside surface.

When von Kleist held the jar and touched its metal rod to a static generator, an immense charge collected on the jar's surface. Von Kleist then discharged it by touching the rod with his hand. In subsequent tests, von Kleist unleashed the jar's electrical force on small children. The jar released enough current to disrupt the electrical signals passing through the children's nerves to control their muscles. The children were knocked off their feet. They were shaken but unharmed.

Other scientists subsequently built their own Leyden jars and subjected themselves to the jars' power. They reported a variety of physical symptoms including temporary breathlessness and paralysis, nosebleeds, concussions, convulsions, and dizziness.

The Leyden jar had two major advantages over static generators. It could hold more charge, and it was more portable. Whereas static generators filled large rooms, Leyden jars were compact and held their charge for days. Suddenly electrical experiments could be conducted anywhere.

Later researchers multiplied the electrical power at their disposal by wiring together a series of Leyden jars. An early Leyden jar assembly preserved in Leyden's Boerhaave Museum has an adjustable dial. Researchers could use the dial to select one of four levels of electrical charge. The dial's settings ran from "detonating cannon" at the low end to "melting wire" at the highest setting.

DuFay and his supporters struggled unsuccessfully to use the two-fluid theory of electricity to explain the

Leyden jar's operation. The solution—ditching the two-fluid theory—would come from an unlikely source, a printer in Philadelphia, Pennsylvania, for whom electricity was a hobby. That printer was Benjamin Franklin.

PACKING A CHARGE

In modern terminology, the Leyden jar is a capacitor—a device that stores electricity and releases it when needed. When a flow of electrons (an electric current) is applied to the jar, electrons pile up on one face of the glass, giving it a negative charge. Let's say the electrons are on the outer surface of the jar. This negative charge pushes electrons away from the jar's inner surface, giving that surface a positive charge. The glass in between separates the positive and negative charges, preventing a current from flowing and thereby storing the charge. To discharge a Leyden jar, you simply use a conductor, such as a metal wire or rod, to connect both surfaces of the jar. The electrons piled on one surface of the jar race through the wire toward the positive charge on the other surface.

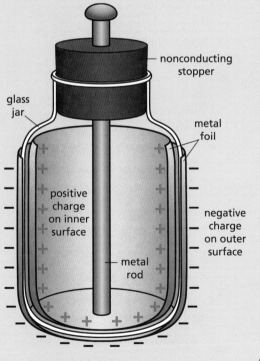

nonconducting stopper

glass jar

metal foil

positive charge on inner surface

metal rod

negative charge on outer surface

CHAPTER 3

FRANKLIN'S FLUID FIRE

Benjamin Franklin was a successful printer and publisher in colonial Philadelphia, Pennsylvania, when he took up electrical experimentation in 1746. Franklin's friend Peter Collinson, a business associate in London, England, sent Franklin a glass tube for generating static electricity and a recent treatise on electrical experiments. Franklin soon became hooked on dabbling with charges.

Before long Franklin devoted himself almost exclusively to scientific exploration. The results advanced electrical science and made Franklin a celebrity at home and abroad.

Franklin's reports of a remarkable kite experiment sealed his reputation as a scientist. Franklin claimed to have flown the kite during a thunderstorm, conveying electricity down a rain-soaked kite string to charge a Leyden jar on the ground and proving that lightning is electricity.

Modern historians of science do not consider Franklin's experiment to be a great breakthrough. Other scientists had noted earlier that static sparks resemble miniature lightning bolts. Besides, Franklin may not have actually conducted his famous kite experiment. As historian Michael Schiffer wrote, "The apparent foolhardiness of this experiment has led some critics to suggest that Franklin never carried it out." A bolt of lightning is extremely dangerous. It carries more electric power than all the power plants in the United States, combined, for the fraction of a second that it exists.

Franklin first wrote of experimenting with lighting in a 1750 letter to his friend Peter Collinson. Franklin sent the letter for presentation to the Royal Society of London—an exclusive club for Great Britain's leading scientists. In this letter, Franklin suggested an experiment to test if lightning is a form of electricity. He recommended using an iron bar 20 to 30 feet (6–9 m) tall to carry lightning down to the ground.

Two years passed before a scientist took up Franklin's suggestion to draw down lightning. Then Georges-Louis Leclerc, a celebrated botanist, erected a 40-foot (12 m) iron pole in a village north of Paris. As Franklin directed, Leclerc insulated the pole from the ground. On May 10, 1752, the village priest heard a thunderclap near the pole and ran to examine the device. A soldier with the priest brought a wine bottle with a brass ring at the neck. Moving the bottle toward the pole, he drew a series of sparks.

Leclerc heralded Franklin as the genius behind the experiment. However, Franklin wanted credit for having proven lightning's electrical nature himself. Franklin's associates said he had conducted his kite experiment that June, before news of Leclerc's experiment reached the colonies, giving Franklin an independent claim on the proof that lightning and electricity are one. But Franklin's own newspaper, the *Pennsylvania Gazette*, did not announce his kite experiment until October 1752, months after the news of Leclerc's demonstration had raced around the world.

Georg Wilhelm Richmann, a German experimenter at Russia's Imperial Academy of Sciences, demonstrated the full danger of Franklin's experiments. Richmann erected an iron rod to convey electricity through a brass chain to a Leyden jar. When lightning struck the rod, the electrical current ripping through the chain destroyed the Leyden jar and killed Richmann, who was seated close to the chain. Witnesses reported that a ball of blue flame jumped 1 foot (0.3 m) from the chain to Richmann's head, killing him instantly.

FRANKLIN DELIVERS

Franklin's brilliant contribution to electrical science was his careful analysis of electrical charges and their movements. Rather than focusing on attraction and repulsion, Franklin sought to explain how objects—including the perplexing Leyden jar—became charged and discharged.

By the mid-eighteenth century, Franklin and many of his European colleagues had come to imagine electricity to be a stream of some sort of charged particles. Unlike the Europeans, however, Franklin saw that the movement of just one type of charged particle, not two, could explain all the electrical experiments to date. Franklin surmised that when an object is rubbed, it either gains or gives up charges. Franklin believed that

DuFay's vitreous charge resulted from an excess of "electrical fire." To Franklin, sparks leaping from a charged object were evidence of this electrical fire. Franklin referred to objects with vitreous charge as positively charged. A deficiency of electrical fire left an object negatively charged.

Franklin described his ideas in a letter to his friend Collinson. "We had for some time been of opinion that the electrical fire was not created by friction, but collected, being really an element diffused among, and attracted by other matter, particularly by water and metals. . . . To electrise plus or minus, no more needs to be known than this, that the parts of the tube or sphere that are rubbed do, in the instant of the friction, attract the electrical fire, and therefore take it from the thing rubbing."

Franklin's idea allowed him to explain electrical transmission. Conductors, he realized, allow the electrical fire to move, while insulators do not. Franklin knew that the particles making up the electrical fire must be tiny. How else could they race through conductors so quickly that they could not be measured? He confidently asserted, "The electrical matter consists of particles extremely subtle, since it can permeate common matter, even the densest metals, with such ease and freedom as not to receive any perceptible resistance."

The most potent proof of Franklin's theories was his explanation of the workings of the Leyden jar. Most scientists assumed that the jar's electrical charge resided in the water inside. Franklin showed that pouring the water from a charged jar into an uncharged jar did not convey its charge. Then he explained why.

Franklin recognized that the charges resided on the surfaces of the jar. One surface had a positive charge (excess electrical fire) and the other had a negative charge (a shortage of electrical fire). The charges endured because glass is an insulator. The glass prevented the electrical fluid from passing from one surface of the jar to the other.

Could Modern Leyden Jars Power Automobiles?

Electrically powered cars, trucks, and buses could one day replace gasoline-powered vehicles. Already automakers sell hybrid vehicles that run on both gasoline and electricity. To make all-electric vehicles, carmakers need to find a way to carry lots of stored electricity on board. One possibility is the ultracapacitor, a modern version of the Leyden jar.

Like the Leyden jar, ultracapacitors store power as static electricity. They can store far more electricity, however, than the Leyden jars of Benjamin Franklin's time, which had just flat surfaces to hold their charge. Ultracapacitors store electric charges on plates of carbon riddled with pores and fissures. This carbon Swiss cheese provides lots of surface area where charges can gather.

Ultracapacitors outperform the conventional batteries that power most electric vehicles. A conventional battery uses chemical reactions to store energy. It wears down a bit each time it is charged. Eventually, it can no longer hold a charge. Ultracapacitors can be charged and discharged millions of times more than batteries before they wear out.

Critics in Europe initially scoffed at Franklin's one-fluid theory. Franklin responded, "If any one should doubt whether the electrical matter passes through the substance of bodies, or only over and along their surfaces, a shock from an electrified large glass jar, taken through his own body, will probably convince him."

Only after Leclerc conducted Franklin's lightning experiment did Franklin receive the acclaim he deserved. Thereafter, Franklin was hailed as the world's leading electrical scientist. He was granted membership in London's Royal Society and the French Academy, France's elite scientific club.

This newfound credibility had global consequences. When the American colonies declared their independence from Great Britain, colonial leaders selected Franklin to serve as their ambassador to France. Franklin negotiated a crucial military alliance with the French. Later, Franklin's diplomacy clinched the treaty in which Great Britain accepted the United States' freedom.

MAGNETISM RETURNS

In the years leading up to the American Revolution (1775–1783) came a profound discovery about the power of electricity. It was made by the British chemist Joseph Priestley, one of the scientists inspired by Franklin's success. This discovery ultimately revealed an intriguing similarity between electricity and magnetism.

Priestley measured the force exerted by electric charges at a given distance. As Gilbert had observed with magnetic forces, Priestley found that the forces between two charged objects grew as he edged them closer together. Furthermore, he found that he could describe the increase in the force with a simple formula based on the distance between the two objects. Cutting the distance in half, Priestley found, produced four times the force. This equation is known as the inverse square law.

Priestley considered his equation too simple to be significant. The idea lay dormant from 1767, when Priestley made the observation, until 1785. In that year, French scientist Charles de Coulomb independently discovered the relationship using a sensitive instrument of his own design called a torsion balance. In this device, a charge hung at the end of a fiber. Repulsion from a second charge caused the fiber to twist until the tension in the twisted fiber equaled the force of repulsion. The degree of twist thereby provided a measure of the force of repulsion.

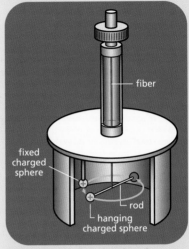

COULOMB'S TORSION BALANCE

fiber

fixed charged sphere

rod

hanging charged sphere

The two charged spheres repel each other. The hanging sphere is pushed away, twisting the fiber.

As a result of his discovery, Coulomb has been immortalized in the units of electrical science. The coulomb is the standard unit used to measure electrical charge.

After rediscovering the inverse square law for electrical force, Coulomb made another intriguing discovery. He found that the inverse square law also applies to magnetic force. If magnetism and electricity follow the same laws, he thought, might they be related?

Scientists had already found intriguing hints of a link between magnetism and electricity. For example, researchers had observed that charged Leyden jars and lightning could both disrupt the magnetization of compasses. In 1681 a vessel struck by lightning in the mid-Atlantic found that its compass had been reoriented so that its south pole pointed toward Polaris. (The ship was navigated successfully to Boston by reading the compass upside down.)

Coulomb proposed a fluid theory of magnetism, adapting Franklin's one-fluid theory of electricity. To explain why magnetism did not produce sparks like electricity, Coulomb proposed that a magnet's moving fluids lay trapped within tiny bits of matter. They therefore could not be transmitted like electricity.

Thanks to Coulomb, magnetism was suddenly relevant to electrical science. But even Coulomb thought that electricity and magnetism resulted from the movements of two distinct types of matter. In the 1800s, scientists would realize that the two phenomena are more closely related than the French physicist could have imagined.

CHAPTER 4

OERSTED'S COMPASS

Readers of the third edition of *Encyclopaedia Britannica*, which was completed in 1797, found more than 120 pages devoted to electrical science. Within half a century, however, they would be reading about electrical engineering—the practical application of electrical science. Electrical scientists would unify electricity with the previously distinct field of magnetism. In the process, they would transform electricity from an entertaining spectacle into an important engineering tool.

Charles de Coulomb's inverse square laws suggested a connection between electricity and magnetism. But it was the invention of the battery by Alessandro Volta in the 1790s that enabled scientists to forge the link. The battery produced a new form of electricity—continuous current. Static electricity simply transfers excess charges from one object to another. Electrical current is the movement of streams of charges, such as electricity flowing through a power cord.

Alessandro Volta became a professor in 1779.

Volta was an ambitious professor of experimental physics at the University of Pavia near Milan in modern-day Italy. He did not set out to make a battery. Rather, his goal was to win an academic debate with Luigi Galvani, a renowned medical professor at nearby Bologna University. Galvani had proposed a theory of animal electricity—the idea that the source of life was a fluid like electricity.

Scientists had long known that a spark from a Leyden jar could cause muscles to contract. Galvani observed the same effect, but without the Leyden jar, as he dissected a frog's leg. As his scalpel cut into the frog, the steel blade happened to touch a brass hook that pinned the frog in place. To Galvani's surprise, the frog's leg twitched. In subsequent experiments, Galvani showed that a frog's legs twitched whenever they were touched with two different kinds of metal at the same time. Since the muscles had moved with no apparent external source of charge, Galvani concluded that the frog's body contained its own form of electricity.

Volta believed the electricity causing the twitching came from the two metals. The frogs' legs, argued Volta, were responding to electricity rather than producing it.

FRANKENSTEIN'S MESSAGE

In 1788 British doctor Charles Kite documented the use of electric discharges to revive victims of drowning and suffocation. Galvani's nephew, Giovanni Aldini, was attempting to use electricity to restore life to dead human bodies by the time British author Mary Shelley published her book *Frankenstein* in 1818.

Aldini conducted his experiments on the corpses of executed criminals. He described a particularly gruesome demonstration where he wired up two severed heads, ear to ear, and an electric shock caused their facial muscles to contract. The eyelids became particularly animated. "Some of the spectators who were not prepared for such results were exceedingly horrified," wrote Aldini.

While electric shocks have yet to produce a real Frankenstein's monster, they are routinely used to revive victims of drowning or suffocation. The electric defibrillator, invented in 1947, has revived thousands of people whose hearts stopped beating.

To prove his point, Volta took life out of the picture entirely. He sandwiched a piece of paper soaked with salt water between zinc and silver discs. Then he ran a wire from one metal disc to the other. An electrometer detected electricity flowing through the wire. Volta's device became known as the voltaic battery.

Volta found that he could amplify the electrical force of his device by stacking many layers of metal and paper. The term *battery* refers to this addition of units. Just as gun batteries employ a line of cannons to multiply their destructive force, Volta's stacks of metal and paper multiplied the current. Volta could add more pairs of discs to increase the electricity without limit.

Volta knew that his battery produced a new form of electricity. The Leyden jar unleashed a quick zap of electricity, but Volta's battery delivered a steady stream.

Volta reported using himself as an experimental guinea pig. He connected a voltaic battery's current of electricity to his chest, eyes, and tongue. As a result, he experienced convulsions and strange vision and taste sensations.

Larger voltaic batteries produced immense power. A battery at the Polytechnic Institute in Paris, built on the order of French emperor Napoleon Bonaparte, filled a large hall. According to one account, Napoleon visited the Polytechnic to inspect his battery. Touching its wires to his tongue, he received a severe shock, temporarily rendering himself "nearly senseless."

Volta's new electrical source prompted a series of new experiments. Chemists experimented with various combinations of metals and liquids and found different gases bubbling out of the liquids. Other researchers investigated the electric power produced by large batteries. British physicist and chemist Humphry Davy used electricity from a battery with two thousand pairs of plates to melt sapphire and evaporate diamond.

Meanwhile, technologists began using the electric current to send signals down a wire. An early telegraph was assembled in 1812. It transmitted coded messages nearly 2 miles (3 kilometers).

PILING ON THE VOLTS

The voltaic battery is a chemical device. It produces electricity because atoms of some metals hold on to their electrons more tightly than others. Placing a pair of metals side by side enables electrons to leave one metal, such as zinc, and move to another that attracts electrons more strongly, such as silver. The metal that loses electrons is called the anode. The metal that gains electrons is called the cathode.

The electrons react with the more electron-hungry metal to form negatively charged metal-oxide ions. Each of the metal-oxide ions causes a water molecule in the electrolyte (the salt water or other fluid in the battery) to split into a positively charged hydrogen ion and a negatively charged hydroxide ion. The hydrogen ion combines with the negatively charged metal-oxide ion and becomes inert (chemically inactive). The hydroxide ion flows through the electrolyte to the anode, where it combines with a positively charged metal ion and produces a water molecule and a metal-oxide molecule. In other words, the anode rusts.

Chemist William Nicholson and surgeon Anthony Carlisle used the voltaic battery to discover electrolysis. This is the electrochemical reaction by which water breaks apart into hydrogen and oxygen gases.

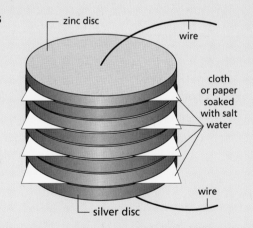

zinc disc

wire

cloth or paper soaked with salt water

wire

silver disc

If the two wires of this voltaic battery are brought into contact, electrons flow from the zinc discs toward the silver discs.

Deflecting the Needle

In the spring of 1820, a Danish physicist and professor named Hans Christian Oersted made the remarkable discovery that finally proved the link between electricity and magnetism. Oersted believed in the unity of nature. As early as 1806, he had suggested that one power produces all natural phenomena, including electricity, magnetism, light, and heat.

Oersted placed a wire above a magnetic compass. Then he connected the ends of the wire to a voltaic battery, causing current to flow through the wire. As Oersted did so, he saw the compass's needle jump so that it was perpendicular to the flow of the current.

In July 1820, Oersted announced the discovery of electromagnetism. He reported that a magnetic circulation always flows around an electric current in a conductor and this flow moves in a specific direction. The right-hand rule shows the direction of Oersted's magnetism. Extend your right arm, and point your thumb up. Now imagine that your thumb is a wire and electricity is flowing upward through it. The magnetic field produced by the electricity circles around your thumb. To find out which way it is running, curl your fingers. They will point in the direction of the circulating magnetic field.

Within days of his initial announcement, Oersted extended his observations. He revealed that the strength of a conductor's magnetic effect depends on the quantity of electricity flowing—the current—rather than the force with which it flows, which we call voltage.

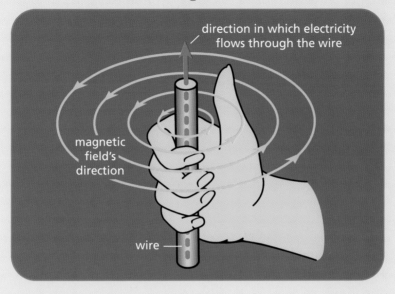

Oersted's Right-Hand Rule

direction in which electricity flows through the wire

magnetic field's direction

wire

André-Marie Ampère, professor of physics at the Collège de France in Paris, witnessed a demonstration of Oersted's electromagnetism at the French Academy on September 11, 1820. After just one feverish week of experimentation and theorizing, Ampère drafted the fundamental laws for the field of electrodynamics (the theory of how electricity and magnets interact). He also built an electromagnet (an electrically powered magnet) and proposed the explanation of magnetism that is still used.

Ampère's key observation was that electric currents can attract and repel one another. The reason is that each current acts like a magnet, and the orientation of its poles depends on the direction of the current's flow. Two currents moving in the same direction are like two magnets that are lined up in the same direction. If they are laid side by side, they will repel each other. Two currents moving in opposite directions will, similarly, attract each other.

To make an electromagnet, Ampère bent a conductor into a spiral. It was essentially a stack of parallel currents with overlapping magnetism. The more twists he made in the wire, the stronger its magnetic field became.

Coulomb had imagined a magnetic fluid circulating within tiny bits of matter inside a magnet. Ampère's theory of magnets, on the other hand, is based on electricity. Ampère imagined tiny electric currents whirring around a magnet's molecules. He said the currents were parallel and circulated in the same direction, like the electricity racing through the coils of an electromagnet. Together, the smaller magnets produced enough magnetism to attract or repel large objects.

In 1822 Ampère derived a mathematical equation that expressed the magnetic force produced by flowing electricity. The equation shows that the magnetic force is proportional to the amount of electrical current. It is also proportional to the number of parallel conductors (or twists in a coil) carrying the current.

Ampère derived his equation using galvanometers, devices that measure electric current. The first galvanometers consisted of a freely turning magnetic needle hung inside a coil of wire. Feeding a current through the coil of wire caused a magnetic field that made the needle rotate. The amount that the needle was deflected depended on the current's strength.

In 1825 German physicist Georg Simon Ohm used the galvanometer to make another fundamental discovery. Ohm found that the current running through a wire increased when he boosted the voltage of the electrical source. In contrast, the current decreased as Ohm increased the resistance (opposition to the flow of current) in the circuit by using thicker wire. Ohm showed mathematically that the amount of current flowing through a circuit equals the voltage divided by the circuit's resistance.

FARADAY'S FIELDS

As scientists unlocked the secrets of electricity and magnetism, technological applications emerged. For example, electricity's magnetic effects provided a way to encode telegraph messages. Send an electric current down a wire, and the resulting magnetic field can be used to deflect a magnetic needle at the other end. To send signals, you simply vary the current. Switching the direction of the electric current three times would cause the needle to flip three times, which could be the signal for a particular word or letter of the alphabet.

While the telegraph sped up the flow of news between distant cities, inventors crammed together more and more coils to produce electromagnets of great strength. In 1831 Joseph Henry unveiled a horseshoe-shaped electro-magnet that could lift objects weighing 750 pounds (340 kilograms). The magnets used to lift scrap iron in modern junkyards employ the same principle.

The most important electromagnetic invention of all was an electromagnet that could spin—the electric motor. Its inventor, Michael Faraday, would also answer the last great unanswered question of electrodynamics. Could magnetism generate electricity, just as electricity could produce magnetism?

Faraday's first motor was very simple. A magnet stood upright in a dish full of the liquid metal mercury, which is an excellent conductor. From above the magnet, Faraday dangled a wire that dipped down into the mer-cury. Faraday connected one pole of a battery to the upper end of the wire and the other to the mercury. This sent a current through the wire and produced a magnetic field around the dangling wire. The dangling wire was continuously attracted or repelled by the magnet's sta-tionary field. The attraction and repulsion caused the wire to rotate around the standing magnet like a horse on a merry-go-round. Reversing the direction of the current reversed the direction of the wire's magnetic field, mak-ing it rotate in the opposite direction. Faraday's motor proved that electricity could be used to do work.

Faraday also demonstrated electromagnetic induction (using magnetism to generate electricity). Most researchers expected a stationary magnet to somehow induce current. Faraday figured that if it took a moving current of electricity to generate magnetism, perhaps some movement of magnetism was required to generate electricity.

Faraday tested his hypothesis with an apparatus consisting of two coils of wire, each wrapped around a portion of the same iron ring. He connected the coil on the left side of the ring to a battery and the coil on the right

Faraday's First Electric Motor

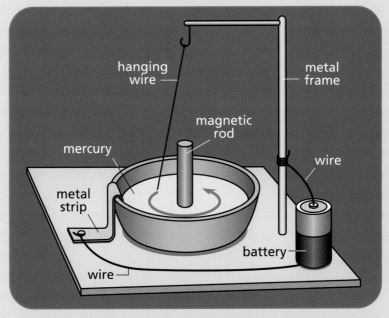

The interaction between the magnetic fields of the hanging wire and the rod causes the wire to rotate around the rod.

side to a galvanometer. By altering the current passing through the left-hand coil and thus changing the iron ring's magnetism, he hoped to produce an electrical current in the right-hand coil. The experiment worked.

Each time Faraday connected the battery to the left-hand coil, a current was induced in the right-hand coil. The effect was brief, however. The needle on Faraday's galvanometer deflected only momentarily, then went back to its original position.

Faraday's Magnetic Induction Experiment

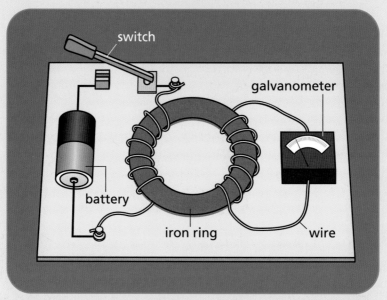

When the switch is closed, current flows through the left-hand coil, inducing a magnetic field around the iron ring. This changing magnetic field causes a momentary current in the right-hand coil.

DEMYSTIFYING THE AURORAS

Swedish astronomer Olof Peter Hiorter established the connection between magnetism and the auroras. Hiorter recorded the position of a compass needle hourly from January 19, 1741, to January 19, 1742. He logged thousands of compass readings and forty appearances of the aurora borealis.

A pattern emerged. Each time the aurora appeared, the compass needle seemed to follow it. At 2:00 P.M. on April 5, 1741, for example, Hiorter watched as the aurora swirled down from the north and swept off to the west. He reported that by 5:18 P.M., the compass needle had moved 2 degrees to the west. As he continued his observations through the night, the aurora receded and the needle edged back to its normal position.

Scientists needed Faraday's notion of electric and magnetic fields to explain this link between the auroras and electricity. In 1896 Norwegian physicist Kristian Olaf Bernhard Birkeland discovered the missing piece of the puzzle—charged particles ejected from storms on the surface of the Sun.

Birkeland reasoned that Earth's magnetic field would carry the charged solar particles toward Earth's poles. The moving charges would excite atoms in Earth's atmosphere and make them glow, much as electricity excites atoms in a neon light. The glowing atoms would cause the aurora's colorful displays.

Birkeland used a magnetized sphere to demonstrate his idea. The sphere simulated Earth's magnetic fields. Birkeland placed the sphere inside a chamber from which the air had been pumped. He blasted the sphere with a beam of electrons and observed that the terrella's magnetic fields steered the electrons toward its magnetic poles. The auroras sweeping down from Earth's poles had been captured in the laboratory.

Faraday recognized that the magnetism caused by the current in the first coil had to be changing to induce a current in the second coil. Faraday did not know the complex math required to describe magnetic forces shifting in space, so he explained electromagnetic induction using images rather than formulas. He visualized electrical and magnetic "force fields."

When metal filings are tossed around a magnet, they arrange themselves in a pattern that follows the magnet's magnetic field. Lines of filings wrap around the magnet's poles. Their density falls off with distance from the magnet, showing that the field's strength decreases with distance.

The iron filings sprinkled on this magnet trace the shape of its magnetic field.

Faraday imagined that his magnetic fields penetrated materials. In his induction experiment, he imagined the magnetic field from the first coil of wire penetrating the second coil of wire. It was the shifting strength of this magnetic field, Faraday believed, that created a shift in the electric field in the second coil. That changing electric field momentarily generated an electromotive force that shoved the electrical charges in the second coil, creating the brief electric current that his electrometer detected.

Faraday's notion of electric and magnetic fields was ignored by most scientists. But the technological applications of Faraday's work were impossible to ignore.

Faraday exploited electromagnetic induction to invent an induction generator that converted mechanical energy into electricity. A mechanical force such as that produced by a waterwheel turned a magnet inside a coil of wire, causing electricity to flow in the wire.

CHAPTER 5

CATCHING WAVES

By the mid-1800s, the field of electrical engineering was in full swing. The first transatlantic telegraph signals raced from London to New York, instantly shrinking the world. Yet the nature of electricity continued to elude scientific explanation. Just what was the electrical "fluid" engineers were pumping under the ocean? Moreover, how did its movement produce magnetism—and vice versa?

Michael Faraday came up with some interesting ideas about magnetic and electric fields. However, he lacked the mathematical skills to convince other scientists. That job fell to James Clerk Maxwell, a young physicist at the University of Cambridge in Great Britain.

Maxwell took up Faraday's ideas in 1854. During the following decade, Maxwell turned Faraday's intuitions into a coherent mathematical theory. In the process, Maxwell showed that electricity and magnetism are more universal than the air we breathe.

SEEING THE LIGHT

Maxwell's genius was in inventing mechanical models to explain Faraday's fields. He imagined the magnetic fields penetrating a material as magnetic rolling pins—the tools used to flatten pastry dough. In Maxwell's model, these pins whirled around in a fluid. He imagined electrical charges as small spheres floating in the fluid between the pins.

James Clerk Maxwell

A steady magnetic field rotated the pins in unison. As a result, the electrical spheres stayed put. In contrast, a shifting magnetic field moving through the material accelerated first some pins and then others. The shifting pins pushed the surrounding fluid around, jostling the spheres.

Next, Maxwell considered conductors and insulators. Electric charges can be carried through a conductor. In Maxwell's rolling-pin model, the spheres in a conductor would move when the magnetic field changed and shifted the fluid around them. The result would be the induced electric current that Michael Faraday had discovered.

Electric charges do not travel through an insulator, however. In his model, Maxwell represented an insulator as a material in which the spheres were stuck in place. A shifting magnetic field would not be able to move them. Nevertheless, Maxwell reasoned that the shifting fluid would exert some strain on the spheres.

Maxwell thought, why not let the spheres change their shape in response to the strain? In physics terminology, why not make the spheres elastic? When the fluid shifted around elastic spheres in an insulator, the spheres would squish like tennis balls. If the fluid pressure squished the spheres, the electric charges would move ever so slightly, causing a small pulse of electrical current. Maxwell called this pulse displacement current.

Maxwell reasoned that, following the known laws of electromagnetic induction, this pulse of displacement current would set off a domino effect. The tiny current would create a tiny magnetic field. The magnetic field, in turn, would induce a tiny electric field, creating a new current. The current would then create another magnetic field. Maxwell called this interaction electricity and magnetism's "mutual embrace." The result would be an electromagnetic wave that traveled through the insulator.

Maxwell then calculated the speed of this electromagnetic wave. To do so, he used the established formula for mechanical forces acting on elastic solids. The formula delivered a mind-blowing result: 193,088 miles per second (310,745 km/sec). The speed of Maxwell's electromagnetic wave was very close to the speed of light, for which the most precise measurement at the time was 195,647 miles per second (314,863 km/sec).

The message was obvious to Maxwell. Light must be an electromagnetic wave.

MAXWELL ADDS IT ALL UP

In 1864 Maxwell published a set of four equations that describe the behavior of electromagnetic radiation. They express Maxwell's insights, as well as the electromagnetic phenomena observed by his predecessors, from Gilbert to Faraday. Maxwell's equations unified electromagnetic science.

Not all scientists immediately embraced Maxwell's ideas. For one thing, he lacked experimental proof. The best instruments of the day could not detect the tiny displacement currents Maxwell predicted.

Maxwell's ideas steadily gained credence over the next two decades, however. During that time, measurements of the speed of light became more accurate and edged closer to the speed Maxwell had calculated. Definite proof finally arrived in 1889, when German physicist Heinrich Hertz produced a new form of electromagnetic wave—radio waves.

Hertz's discovery of radio waves marks the dawn of the wireless age. Broadcasters began using equipment like Hertz's to transmit music and up-to-the minute news on AM radio. Here's how it works. A newscaster speaking in a studio creates sound waves that vibrate an electromagnet in a microphone. The moving magnet generates a fluctuating electric current. An antenna converts the fluctuating current into an electromagnetic wave—a radio wave—that travels through air at the speed of light. When the radio wave hits the antenna on a radio, the wave induces a fluctuating current. That current is amplified to power the radio's speakers, where an electromagnet vibrates the air to reproduce the newscaster's voice.

Hertz proved experimentally that his electromagnetic radio waves moved at the speed of light. After Hertz's demonstration, scientists universally accepted Maxwell's theory of electromagnetic waves. Over the following decades, scientists would detect and produce a wide range of electromagnetic waves. They are considered to be part of an infinitely large continuum of electromagnetic waves called the electromagnetic spectrum.

You experience the different "bands" of electromagnetic waves, or radiation, all the time. A band is a set of waves defined by their wavelength—the distance between neighboring peaks in the wave. The shorter the wavelength, the more often the wave oscillates (moves back and forth). The rate of oscillation is called the fre-

The Electromagnetic Spectrum

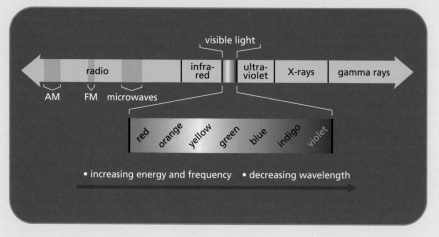

quency. Radiation with shorter wavelengths packs more energy than radiation with longer wavelengths.

Visible light is the band of electromagnetic waves the human eye can detect. Bands with longer wavelengths include the infrared waves, which are felt as heat, and Hertz's radio waves, which we can't detect at all—until we crank up a radio. Bands of lower wavelengths include the ultraviolet radiation that causes sunburn and x-rays used to spot broken bones.

Maxwell's math predicted the behavior of all of these electromagnetic waves. But it did not explain what electromagnetic waves move through. In the ocean, waves travel by pushing molecules of water up and down along the way. What, wondered Maxwell, do electromagnetic waves move up and down and back and forth as they travel? A young scientist from Germany, Albert Einstein, would soon convince scientists that the question was irrelevant. In the process, he would develop a whole new concept of time and space.

CHAPTER 6

THE NEW PHYSICS

By the late 1800s, physicists were hot on the trail of the charged particle that Benjamin Franklin had envisioned as the source of electricity 150 years earlier. In 1874 Irish physicist George Johnstone Stoney was studying electrolysis—breaking a chemical compound into its elements by subjecting it to electric current. Specifically, Stoney was using electrolysis to turn water into oxygen and hydrogen gases.

Stoney found that a certain quantity of electricity was needed to break apart each molecule of water. From this he calculated that there was a fundamental charge equal to roughly 100 quintillionths of a coulomb. That's such a small amount of electricity that it might take 10,000 trillion of Stoney's charges to deliver a static shock on a winter day. In 1891 Stoney named this tiny, fundamental charge the electron.

During the same period, physicists were trying to puzzle out the workings of the cathode ray tube—the technological predecessor of a television picture tube. A cathode ray tube is a glass tube connected to an electric current. A platinum plate inserted at one end of the tube serves as the negative terminal, or cathode. A metal plate at the far end serves as the positive terminal, or anode.

It was named a cathode ray tube because when scientists pumped the air out of it and turned on the current, a continuous glowing ray shot out from the cathode to the anode. These rays were perplexing. Unlike light and other electromagnetic radiation, they could be deflected by a magnetic field. But unlike particles, they passed straight through pieces of thin metal foil.

In 1897 British physicist J. J. Thomson, a professor at the University of Cambridge, solved the mystery. Thomson showed that cathode rays were a stream of electrons.

The Cathode Ray Tube

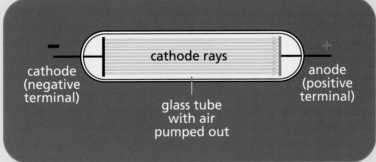

cathode rays

cathode
(negative
terminal)

anode
(positive
terminal)

glass tube
with air
pumped out

When the cathode and anode are connected to an electric current, glowing cathode rays shoot from the cathode to the anode.

Prior to 1897, experiments by Thomson and others had shown that both magnetic fields and electric fields deflected cathode rays and that the rays appeared to be negatively charged. Thomson's breakthrough was to hit the rays with magnetic and electric fields simultaneously. He used a magnetic field of known strength to deflect a cathode ray from its straight path. Then he applied an electric field to pull the stream of light back to center. As he did so, he measured precisely how much electrical force was required.

Thomson knew that the electric and magnetic fields had exerted equal force on the cathode ray, because each field had exactly counteracted the effect of the other. Using Maxwell's equations, he calculated the ratio of the mass of each of the ray's particles to the charge on each particle. The ratio could be interpreted two ways. If the mystery particle weighed the same as the smallest known atom, hydrogen, it had an immense charge. If, on the other hand, the particle carried Stoney's fundamental charge, its mass was very small—only one-thousandth the mass of a hydrogen atom. Thomson guessed, correctly, that the latter was the case. The particle's small size accounted for the cathode rays' ability to pass through metal foils.

American physicist Robert Millikan later confirmed Thomson's guess. Millikan measured the tiny charge on individual electrons at -1.609×10^{-19} coulombs (just slightly bigger than Stoney's estimate). The best modern measurements of the electron peg its charge at -1.6022×10^{-19} coulombs.

DC Versus AC In the 1880s and 1890s, two types of electric power systems battled for supremacy in the United States—direct current (DC) and alternating current (AC). Each had a feisty industrial champion.

Thomas Edison backed DC, which pushes electricity down a wire in a continuous stream. Edison's power station distributed electricity at a fixed voltage. To serve more customers, Edison had to increase the amount of current. But that caused power to be lost from the lines.

Edison's rival, George Westinghouse, backed AC, which conducts electricity by yanking electrons back and forth rather than circulating them in one direction. AC became very attractive in 1881, when Lucian Gaulard and J. D. Gibbs exhibited a device called a transformer. It could increase or decrease the voltage on a power line—but it only worked with AC power.

The transformer has two coils of wire. AC power fed through one coil creates a shifting magnetic field. The changing field induces a current in the second coil, which has a different number of turns of wire. If the second coil has twice as many turns as the first, the voltage increases by a factor of two.

With the transformer, one could generate electricity at low voltage, then transform it to thousands of volts for transmission. The high-voltage electricity had a very low current, so it could travel a long distance with minimal loss of power. A second transformer at the other end of the line could step down the voltage for delivery to customers.

In 1896 Edison's company paid Westinghouse for the right to use his AC technology. AC has been the dominant power system ever since.

RETURN OF THE ATOM

Thomson's measurements of the electron crystallized the development of the modern theory of the atom. Scientists had found that electrons seemed to come out of atoms when they were zapped with electricity. Thomson theorized that each atom contained a distinct number of electrons, starting with hydrogen, which has just one electron. He thought that the electrons were mixed into a much larger dollop of matter, like raisins blended into pudding. The electrons' negative charges would be balanced by an equal but positive charge in the "pudding" surrounding them, which also contributed most of the atom's mass.

Thomson's student, the New Zealander Ernest J. Rutherford, proposed an alternative model. In Rutherford's model, the electrons orbit like satellites around a positively charged nucleus. This model explained how electrons might cause magnetism. The charged electrons whizzing around each nucleus would represent an electric current. According to Faraday's rules, they would induce a magnetic field. In other words, atoms were the tiny electromagnets that Ampère had imagined.

In most materials, the electrons in neighboring atoms would orbit every which way, so their magnetic fields would cancel each other out. But in a magnet, the electrons would orbit parallel to one another. The many tiny magnetic fields would combine to produce a much larger magnetic field, just as multiple coils increase the strength of an electromagnet.

Rutherford's model also explained electricity. Energy added to a material would speed up its orbiting electrons until they broke free of their atoms. The movement of the negatively charged electrons would generate an electromagnetic wave that would speed through the conductor. The wave would energize other electrons in its path.

A FINE YEAR FOR PHYSICS

Just when the theory of electromagnetic waves seemed to be solidifying, German physicist Albert Einstein pulled the rug out from under it. In 1905 Einstein wrote four scientific papers that resulted in a radical reconstruction of physics.

In the first paper, Einstein challenged Maxwell's ideas about light. He showed that although light travels through open space like a wave, it collides with matter like a particle.

A first step in this direction had come from German theorist Max Planck. Planck had derived an equation showing that electromagnetic waves could be released only in distinct bundles of energy. Planck called these energy bundles quanta.

Einstein's first 1905 paper built on Planck's work to explain a phenomenon known as the photoelectric effect. When electromagnetic waves strike metal, they sometimes knock free some of the metal's electrons. If light is a wave, increasing the intensity of the light should push those electrons with more energy. But it doesn't. Instead, increasing the intensity of the light merely unleashes more electrons, each of which has the same amount of energy.

Light waves, Einstein theorized, must be made up of distinct particles of energy like Planck's quanta. He called these light particles photons. The energy of a photon is inversely proportional to its wavelength—the shorter the wavelength, the greater the photon's energy.

Einstein's explanation of the photoelectric effect would later win him the Nobel Prize in Physics. But it was Einstein's 1905 paper on the theory of special relativity that would amaze the world.

Scientists were still trying to understand what light and other electromagnetic waves travel through. The waves in a pond, for example, travel through water. The space between galaxies, in contrast, seems to be a perfect vacuum containing absolutely nothing. How is it, then, that we can see light from distant galaxies?

In 1887 American physicists Albert Abraham Michelson and Edward Morley had attempted to answer this question. They had conducted experiments to try to find out whether space is filled with an invisible substance, known as the ether, that light moves through. Michelson and Morley reasoned that, if this hidden ether exists, Earth must travel through it as it rotates around the Sun. Therefore light beamed from Earth in the direction of Earth's orbit should encounter ether rushing toward it—an ether headwind. Just as a headwind slows down a bicyclist, they figured this ether wind should slow down a light wave. Similarly, light waves beamed from Earth in the opposite direction should encounter an ether tailwind and speed up. Light waves traveling in other directions should also speed up or slow down, but to a lesser degree.

Directly measuring the speed of light wasn't an option. Light travels mind-blowingly fast, and any change in speed due to an ether wind was expected to be extremely small—too small to be detected using the best equipment then available. Michelson and Morley's experiment instead took an indirect approach.

The partners used a partially silvered mirror to split a beam of light. Half of the beam shot straight through, and the other half was deflected at a right angle. Mirrors then bounced the two beams back and forth several times before aiming both into a single eyepiece. When two sets of waves meet, they produce an interference pattern, such as when two sets of ripples meet in a pond. This interference pattern would be visible in the eyepiece. If there was an ether, the interference pattern would change depending on the direction of the original light beam. To eliminate vibrations that could blur the interference pattern, Michelson and Morley put their apparatus on a solid block of marble. They floated the entire setup in a pool of mercury so it could be turned in any direction.

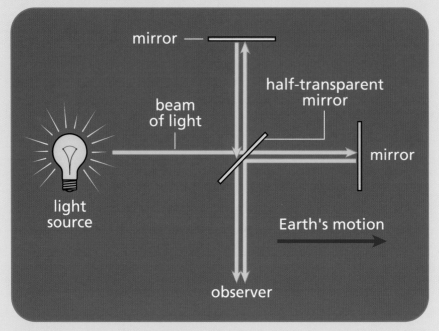

The Michelson-Morley Experiment

mirror

half-transparent mirror

beam of light

mirror

light source

Earth's motion

observer

If light is a wave traveling through ether, then the speed of the beam traveling in the same direction as Earth should be changed, but the speed of the other beam should not.

Michelson and Morley conducted their experiment over and over, pointing the beam in various directions in search of a change caused by the ether. The beam of light always traveled at the same speed. They found no evidence that the ether existed.

If there is no ether, how do electromagnetic waves travel through space? Einstein said the question is irrelevant. We must simply accept that they do, because that is what our experiments show.

Similarly, we must accept that the speed of light is constant. Einstein's theory of special relativity describes a universe in which light always moves at a constant speed relative to any observer's frame of reference.

Einstein found that when he pinned down the speed of light, time and space began to shift. Consider two perfectly synchronized clocks. You hold one, and your friend jumps on a rocket with the second. The rocket takes off at nearly the speed of light. With a telescope, you keep an eye on your friend's clock. According to special relativity, your friend's clock will appear to run more slowly than yours as it is carried off into space. To your friend in his rocket, however, his clock seems to run perfectly.

The reason you have never seen clocks speeding up and slowing down in your daily life is that we don't move anywhere near the speed of light. At slower speeds, the effect of special relativity is very small. You'd need a very special clock to measure it.

Satellites move fast enough compared with Earth's surface to experience the time changes Einstein predicted. Two dozen Global Positioning System (GPS) satellites orbit Earth at 2.4 miles per second (3.9 km/sec). Signals broadcast from the satellites enable people on the ground to determine their exact location anywhere on Earth. To remain precisely synchronized, the satellites must adjust for the slowing of their clocks (relative to clocks on the ground) caused by their flight speed. The adjustment is small—about 0.0072 seconds per day—but without it the system would no longer work. Such adjustments have become standard business for physicists.

SUPERCONDUCTORS In 1911 Dutch scientist Heike Onnes made a startling discovery. When he cooled mercury to a frigid –452°F (–269°C)—only a few degrees above absolute zero, the lowest temperature possible—the metal's resistance to the flow of electricity vanished. Onnes had discovered superconductivity.

The discovery offered an amazing potential for engineering. Superconducting metal could carry immense currents of electricity, creating giant magnetic fields. Those fields could power incredibly strong motors or levitate heavy devices such as trains.

The problem for engineers is maintaining a temperature just above absolute zero. Keeping something that cool requires liquid helium refrigeration equipment, which uses lots of electricity. To make superconducting machines practical, scientists would have to invent a superconductor that worked at warmer temperatures.

A major breakthrough came in 1986. IBM researchers discovered ceramic materials that are superconductors at temperatures as high as –218°F (–139°C). That temperature may sound very cold, but it can be reached by bathing the superconducting machines in liquid nitrogen, which is much cheaper than liquid helium.

Superconductive materials continue to pose a challenge for engineers because, like most ceramics, they are stiff. They make brittle wires. However, companies are already using them to develop the first generation of superconducting motors.

CHAPTER 7

MODERN MYSTERIES

In the decades that followed 1905, physicists discovered that light is not the only substance to behave like both a wave and a particle. All matter leads this dual existence. The mathematics used to describe this new concept of matter is called quantum mechanics.

Well into the 1940s, quantum mechanics had a fatal flaw. In certain situations, it did not provide reasonable answers. For example, the theory seemed to show that electrons sometimes have infinite energy. It predicted a feedback loop whenever an electron moved. Some of the electromagnetic waves produced by the electron would reflect off neighboring particles and bounce back, moving the electron some more. Once set in motion, this feedback loop would seem to keep the electron hopping forever, releasing an infinite amount of energy.

The notion of an electron producing an infinite stream of energy did not sit well with Einstein's theory of special relativity. Special relativity showed that an electron with infinite energy would also have infinite mass. J. J. Thomson had proved that this was false when he measured the finite mass of the electron.

California Institute of Technology professor Richard Feynman used Einstein's theory of relativity to fix the flaw in quantum mechanics. Feynman's solution was to simply forbid any charged particle from acting on itself. He assumed that half of the electron's radiation had bounced off the neighboring particles a moment after it jiggled, as one would expect. The other half, he assumed, had bounced off the neighboring particles a moment *before* the jiggle. The electron did this by producing electromagnetic waves that traveled both forward and backward in time. This strange behavior was permitted by quantum mechanics, but few scientists before Feynman had been willing to consider it.

Feynman's proposal solved the problem. The two sets of reflected electromagnetic radiation arriving back at the electron cancel each other out. As a result, the electron does not keep jiggling forever.

Feynman made no apologies for the weird sense of time and space employed in his theory, which is known as quantum electrodynamics. "The theory of quantum electrodynamics describes Nature as absurd from the point of view of common sense," said Feynman. "And it fully agrees with experiment. So I hope you can accept Nature as She is—absurd."

Feynman published the final version of his quantum electrodynamics equations in 1947. Since then, scientists employing similar techniques have predicted the many

The Tevatron *(above)* is housed in a circular tunnel. A water-filled trench follows the outside of the tunnel. It keeps the accelerator's magnets cool.

subatomic particles that make up an atom's nucleus and the forces that hold them together. To observe these particles, scientists have unleashed the contents of atomic nuclei by smashing particles together in giant machines called particle accelerators.

Particle accelerators use powerful electromagnets to accelerate charged particles. The Tevatron in Batavia, Illinois, the world's most powerful particle accelerator, whips protons around an underground ring that is 4 miles (6.4 km) in circumference. The magnets then guide the protons into head-on collisions, blowing them apart and unleashing immense energy.

Two Steps Forward . . .

Scientists continue to debate the fundamental validity of Feynman's mathematics. Even Feynman had his doubts. In mathematical terms, quantum electrodynamics solved the problem of infinitely energetic and massive electrons by subtracting one infinite calculation from another. Physicists are suspicious of this mathematical trick.

Sixty years later, no one truly understands why Feynman's mathematical sleight of hand works or what his equations truly represent. For all its insights into the nature of the atom, quantum electrodynamics falls far short of Faraday's fields or Maxwell's elastic spheres as a way of visualizing electromagnetism.

String theory is one of the most advanced efforts to push beyond quantum electrodynamics. It is an attempt to unify the four currently recognized forces of nature. These forces are electromagnetism, gravity, the strong force that holds the atomic nucleus together, and the weak force that causes some kinds of radioactivity.

String theory unifies the four fundamental forces by imagining a world composed of vibrating loops of "string." These loops are so small that they make electrons look big. According to string theory, their vibrations add up to much more, the way individual notes on a guitar resonate to form a chord.

String theory has not yet been proven by experiment. Worse still, say critics, because the strings predicted by the theory would be so small, they would be beyond the reach of experimentation!

STORMY FUTURE

Many questions about electromagnetism remain to be answered. For example, some physicists are searching for magnetic particles that behave like electric charges. Imagine a magnet with one pole instead of two and you'll get an inkling of how different those particles would be.

Other scientists are exploring new electromagnetic phenomena on Earth and above it. Consider the recent discovery of terrestrial gamma rays. Gamma rays are high-energy packets of electromagnetic energy. In 1925 Charles Wilson, a Nobel prize-winning British physicist, had predicted they might be found on Earth. He had proposed that gamma rays might appear after some lightning discharges. But until recently, the only gamma rays detected were thought to be those created by catastrophic cosmic events, such as the collapse of a star to form a black hole.

Most lightning strikes shoot negative charges to the ground. Less commonly, the positively charged upper part of a cloud discharges a positive lightning bolt. After such positive cloud-to-ground strikes, thunderclouds are momentarily packed with negative charges. Wilson predicted that a dramatic chain reaction would take place in negatively charged clouds. First, the negative charges would create a brief electric field stretching high into the sky. That electric field would draw electrons out of the cloud, shooting them skyward. These electrons would collide with atoms in the air, causing them to release powerful gamma rays.

The gamma rays Wilson predicted were confirmed in 1991 by an orbiting satellite telescope. The satellite observed several bursts of cosmic gamma rays each day.

About once each month, its instruments also picked up gamma rays from Earth. The bursts were much shorter in duration than the cosmic gamma rays. As a result, the satellite's sensors couldn't accurately read their strength.

In 2002 the National Aeronautics and Space Administration launched a new satellite carrying an instrument designed to study the short bursts of gamma rays from Earth. In February 2005, physicist David Smith used the satellite's data to reveal that the gamma-ray bursts are one hundred times as powerful as previously estimated. They are also far more common than expected. Smith estimates that approximately fifty gamma-ray blasts emanate from Earth's atmosphere daily.

CREATIVE GENIUS

The next question for scientists such as David Smith is where the high-flying electrons released from storm clouds go after they shoot up into the sky. Solving such mysteries requires plenty of specialized knowledge. But as Smith's predecessors showed, scientific discovery requires a lot more than just book learning.

The pioneers of electricity and magnetism were a varied bunch. What they shared was an open mind that enabled them to see beyond the accepted wisdom of their time. Franklin saw that one electrical fluid explained electrical attraction and repulsion better than two. Einstein welcomed the relativity of space and time because it explained experimental observations of light. Roll up your sleeves and open your mind and you might just solve a few mysteries of your own.

ARE ELECTRICAL BLACKOUTS INEVITABLE?

Plenty of electrical engineering mysteries remain to be unraveled. Consider electrical blackouts such as the August 2003 blackout that darkened much of the northeastern United States and central Canada. Some mathematicians, physicists, and engineers believe that blackouts are a natural part of the power system. A blackout, they argue, is the feedback signal that convinces power companies to repair and strengthen their power lines.

It may be possible to fix the power grid and prevent future blackouts, but don't count on it anytime soon. The power grid is incredibly complex. Some engineers believe that a fail-safe check against blackouts may be impossible. Better keep a flashlight handy, and don't forget the batteries!

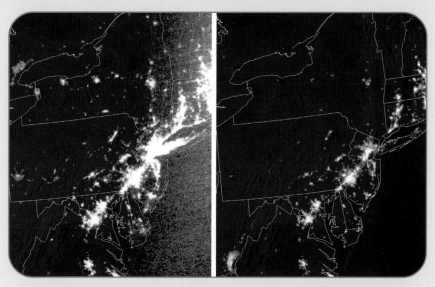

Satellite views of the northeastern United States before *(left)* and during *(right)* the 2003 electrical blackout

GLOSSARY

alternating current (AC): electricity produced by electrons moving back and forth in a circuit. The electric power coming from wall outlets is AC.

amber: fossilized tree sap. Rubbed amber has a static charge.

anode: the negatively charged terminal on a battery

auroras: colorful bands of light that appear in the sky near Earth's poles. They are caused by charged particles from the Sun interacting with Earth's magnetic field.

battery: a chemical device that produces electricity; also called a voltaic battery

capacitor: a device that stores electricity and releases it when needed

cathode: the positively charged terminal on a battery

conductor: a material that transports electric charge efficiently

coulomb: the standard unit of electrical charge

current: a flow of electric charges, measured in amperes (amps)

direct current (DC): electricity that flows continuously in one direction. Batteries produce DC current.

electrical engineering: the practical application of electrical science

electricity: energy resulting from the flow of charged particles, such as electrons

electrodynamics: the theory of how electricity and magnets interact

electromagnet: an electrically powered magnet

electromagnetic spectrum: the entire range of electromagnetic radiation, from the longest wavelengths (radio waves) to the shortest wavelengths (gamma rays)

electrons: negatively charged particles in atoms

ether: the weightless, transparent, frictionless substance nineteenth-century scientists thought filled the universe, providing a medium through which light waves could travel

gamma rays: high-energy packets of electromagnetic energy

grounded: connected to the ground

induction: using a changing magnetic field to produce an electric current in a conductor

insulator: a material that is a poor conductor of electricity

Leyden jar: a device for storing electricity

magnetic field: area of magnetic force that exists around a magnet or a current-carrying conductor

magnetite: a mineral that is a natural magnet; also known as lodestone

photons: individual packets of electromagnetic energy; particles of light

quantum (pl. quanta): the smallest unit of energy. A quantum of light is called a photon.

quantum mechanics: the study of the behavior of the particles that make up the atomic nucleus; also called quantum physics

resistance: the degree to which a material slows the flow of electric current

static electricity: the buildup of electric charges on a surface

transformer: a device used to increase or decrease the voltage on an AC power line

voltage: the force that causes an electric current to flow; also known as electromotive force

wavelength: the distance from one peak of a wave to the next

TIMELINE

CA. **7000** B.C.	Prehistoric people carve animal figures from amber.
A.D. **70**	Pliny the Elder comments on magnetism.
CA. **1150**	European mariners begin to use compasses for navigation.
1600	William Gilbert publishes *On the Magnet*.
1729	Stephen Gray discovers the principles of electrical conduction.
1733	Charles DuFay formulates his two-fluid theory of electricity.
1745–1746	Ewald von Kleist invents the Leyden jar.
1752	Georges-Louis Leclerc, inspired by Benjamin Franklin, proves that lightning is electricity.
1785	Charles de Coulomb proposes his inverse square laws for electrical charge and magnetism, linking electricity and magnetism.
1800	Alessandro Volta announces his invention of the first chemical battery.
1818	Mary Wollstonecraft Shelley's book *Frankenstein* is published.
1820	Hans Christian Oersted discovers the magnetic field produced by a changing current.
1821	Michael Faraday invents the first electric motor.
1831	Faraday discovers electromagnetic induction.
1858	The first telegraph message is sent across the Atlantic Ocean.
1864	James Clerk Maxwell proposes that light is an electromagnetic wave.
1881	The Edison Lamp Company opens its first power station.

1889	Heinrich Hertz produces radio waves.
1897	J. J. Thomson shows that cathode rays are streams of electrons.
1905	Albert Einstein publishes four scientific papers that reshape physical science.
1911	Heike Onnes discovers superconductivity.
1947	Richard Feynman publishes equations that unite special relativity and quantum mechanics.
1986	IBM researchers discover ceramic materials that are superconductors at temperatures much higher than absolute zero.
2005	Terrestrial gamma-ray bursts are found to be one hundred times as powerful as previous estimates.
2007	Saint Louis University researchers announce the development of a battery powered by sugar.

Biographies

André-Marie Ampère (1775–1836) André-Marie Ampère, born in Lyon, France, developed a passion for mathematics at the age of thirteen. He nearly gave it up, however, after French revolutionaries executed his father in 1792. Ampère contributed to mathematics, chemistry, and the theory of light. Then, in 1820, he made his landmark discoveries on the force of magnetic fields generated by electricity. The ampere, the standard unit of electric current, bears his name.

Charles de Coulomb (1736–1806) Physicist Charles de Coulomb was born in Angoulême, France. He served nearly thirty years as an engineer with the French military. In 1789 he retired from the military to pursue scientific research full-time. Coulomb invented sensitive new instruments that led to advances in electricity, magnetism, and the physics of friction. The standard unit of electric charge, the coulomb, was named in his honor.

Albert Einstein (1879–1955) Albert Einstein was born in Ulm, Germany. He earned mediocre grades in college due to a habit of skipping lectures. As a result, he was lucky to land his first job in the patent office in Bern, Switzerland. In 1905 Einstein published a series of important scientific papers that introduced the world to a revolutionary theory of light and the concepts of special and general relativity. He won the Nobel Prize in Physics in 1921 for his work on the photoelectric effect. Einstein, a Jew, moved to the United States in 1933, when Adolf Hitler came to power in Germany. He became a professor of theoretical physics at Princeton University in New Jersey.

Michael Faraday (1791–1867) Faraday was born in Newington, Great Britain. The son of a blacksmith, he rose to become president of Britain's Royal Society. He lacked formal education in mathematics but had excellent intuition and was a keen observer. In 1831 Faraday discovered electromagnetic induction—the production of an electric current by a moving magnetic field. He also was an important inventor. He created the first electric motor and the first generator to produce electric current.

RICHARD FEYNMAN (1918–1988) Feynman was born in New York City. He was fascinated with science and puzzles from an early age. In school, rather than learn trigonometry from his geometry textbook, he derived the formulas himself. He created an entirely new way of looking at electromagnetism that combined Einstein's special relativity with quantum mechanics. He was known for his practical jokes. While working on the atomic bomb during World War II (1939–1945), Feynman made a hobby of cracking open the top-secret safes protecting the U.S. military's nuclear secrets. Toward the end of his career, he led an investigation into the accident that destroyed the space shuttle *Challenger* in 1986.

BENJAMIN FRANKLIN (1706–1790) Franklin was born in Boston, Massachusetts. He became an apprentice to an older brother who ran a printing press. After a falling out with his brother, Franklin ran away to Philadelphia. There he built a successful printing business of his own. Franklin is most famous for experiments that proved that lightning was a form of electricity, but his greater achievement was developing the theory of positive and negative electrical charges. Franklin's scientific fame made him an effective diplomat in Europe, where he gained France's support for American independence.

WILLIAM GILBERT (1544–1603) William Gilbert was born in Colchester, northeast of London, England. He served as royal physician to Britain's Queen Elizabeth I. In 1600 he published a treatise on magnetism and static electricity that is one of the world's first scientific textbooks. In a painting that hangs in Colchester's town hall, Gilbert appears with Queen Elizabeth, demonstrating electrical attraction by levitating what looks like a small feather above a plate. Gilbert died of the plague in 1603.

STEPHEN GRAY (1666–1736) Gray was a cloth dyer born in Canterbury, England. As an elderly man, he lived at the London Charterhouse, a retirement home. There he made his greatest discoveries. Gray demonstrated the transmission of electric charge and discovered insulators. His breakthroughs earned him membership in the Royal Society of London.

HANS CHRISTIAN OERSTED (1777–1851) Oersted was born in Rudkoebing, Denmark. He studied pharmacy, but in 1801 he received a travel scholarship and spent three years exploring Europe. In Germany he met physicist Johann Ritter, who was searching for a link between electricity and magnetism. Oersted made that discovery himself nineteen years later. He discovered the magnetic field that results from a changing electric current. Oersted was also active in literary and political affairs. In Denmark he is revered for promoting the idea that all children—rich or poor—should be educated.

ALESSANDRO VOLTA (1745–1827) Volta was born in Como, Lombardy (modern-day Italy). He determined early in life to make physics his profession. As a teenager, he corresponded with leading electrical experimenters in Europe. By 1779 he was a professor of experimental physics at the University of Pavia, near modern-day Milan. French emperor Napoleon Bonaparte admired Volta and became his patron. Volta is best known for inventing the voltaic battery, a chemical device that produces electricity.

Source Notes

7   Pliny the Elder, "The Natural History: Book XXXVII. The Natural History of Precious Stones," *Perseus Digital Library Project*, n.d., http://www.perseus.tufts.edu/cgibin/ptext?doc=Perseus%3Atext%3A1999.02.0137%3Ahead%3D%232574 (February 26, 2007).

19   Patricia Fara, *An Entertainment for Angels: Electricity in the Enlightenment* (Cambridge, UK: Icon Books, 2002), p. 56.

22   Michael B. Schiffer, *Draw the Lightning Down: Benjamin Franklin and Electrical Technology in the Age of Enlightenment* (Berkeley: University of California Press, 2003), p. 311.

24   Benjamin Franklin, *Franklin's Experiments and Observations on Electricity,* edited by I. Bernard Cohen (Cambridge, MA: Harvard University Press, 1941), pp. 174–175.

26   Ibid., p. 213.

31   Giovanni Aldini, quoted in Schiffer, p. 130.

32   Bern Dibner, *Oersted and the Discovery of Electromagnetism* (New York: Blaisdell Publishing, 1962), p. 12.

46   James Clerk Maxwell, quoted in David Bodanis, *E=mc²: A Biography of the World's Most Famous Equation* (New York: Walker, 2000), p. 47.

62   Richard P. Feynman, *QED: The Strange Theory of Light and Matter* (Princeton, NJ: Princeton University Press, 1988), p. 10.

Selected Bibliography

Bodanis, David. *E=mc²: A Biography of the World's Most Famous Equation*. New York: Walker, 2000.

Einstein, Albert, and Leopold Infeld. *The Evolution of Physics, from Early Concepts to Relativity and Quanta*. New York: Simon and Schuster, 1966.

Feynman, Richard P. *QED: The Strange Theory of Light and Matter*. Princeton, NJ: Princeton University Press, 1988.

Franklin, Benjamin. *Franklin's Experiments and Observations on Electricity*. Edited by I. Bernard Cohen. Cambridge, MA: Harvard University Press, 1941.

Gilbert, William. *De Magnete*. Translated by P. Fleury Mottelay. New York: Dover Publications, 1958.

Lightman, Alan. *Great Ideas in Physics*. New York: McGraw-Hill, 1992.

Meyer, Herbert W. *A History of Electricity and Magnetism*. Cambridge, MA: MIT Press, 1971.

Verschuur, Gerrit L. *Hidden Attraction: The Mystery and History of Magnetism*. New York: Oxford University Press, 1993.

Further Reading

Aczel, Amir D. *The Riddle of the Compass: The Invention That Changed the World*. New York: Harcourt, 2001.

Bodanis, David. *Electric Universe: The Shocking True Story of Electricity*. New York: Crown Publishers, 2005.

Fleisher, Paul. *Waves: Principles of Light, Electricity, and Magnetism*. Minneapolis: Twenty-First Century Books, 2002.

Herbst, Judith. *Relativity*. Minneapolis: Twenty-First Century Books, 2007.

Souza, D. M. *Northern Lights*. Minneapolis: Lerner Publications Company, 1993.

Streissguth, Tom. *Benjamin Franklin*. Minneapolis: Twenty-First Century Books, 2002.

WEBSITES

The Discovery of the Electron
http://www.aip.org/history/electron/
This online exhibit chronicles J. J. Thompson's famous
cathode ray tube experiments.

The Electric Ben Franklin
http://www.ushistory.org/franklin/index.htm
Explore Franklin the printer, scientist, and diplomat through
historic documents, stories, interactive games, streaming
videos, and more.

The Great Magnet, the Earth
http://istp.gsfc.nasa.gov/earthmag/demagint.htm
Learn the science and stories behind Walter Gilbert's
influential experiments.

Atomic Firsts
http://www.sciencemuseum.org.uk/onlinestuff/stories/
atomic_firsts.aspx
Find out how J. J. Thomson and Ernest Rutherford puzzled
out the electron and its place in the atom.

INDEX

PHOTO ACKNOWLEDGMENTS

The images in this book are used with the permission of:
The Art Archive/Private Collection London, p. 9; AIP Emilio
Segre Visual Archives, Brittle Books Collection, p. 30; ©
Francoise Sauze/Photo Researchers, Inc., p. 42; ©
Bettmann/CORBIS, p. 45; © David Parker/Photo Researchers,
Inc., p. 63; © Reuters/CORBIS, p. 67.

Illustrations on pp. 20, 27, 33, 35, 39, 40, 48, 51, 58 by © Laura
Westlund/Independent Picture Service.
Cover illustration by © Tim Parlin/Independent Picture Service